BOOKWORMS

Go, Critter, Go!
Crawl, Ladybug, Crawl!

¡Vamos criaturita, vamos!
¡Trepa mariquita, trepa!

Dana Meachen Rau

Marshall Cavendish
Benchmark
New York

D1543410

Ladybugs have
black spots.

❖

Las mariquitas tienen
manchas negras.

Ladybugs have
red spots.

———◆———

Las mariquitas tienen
manchas rojas.

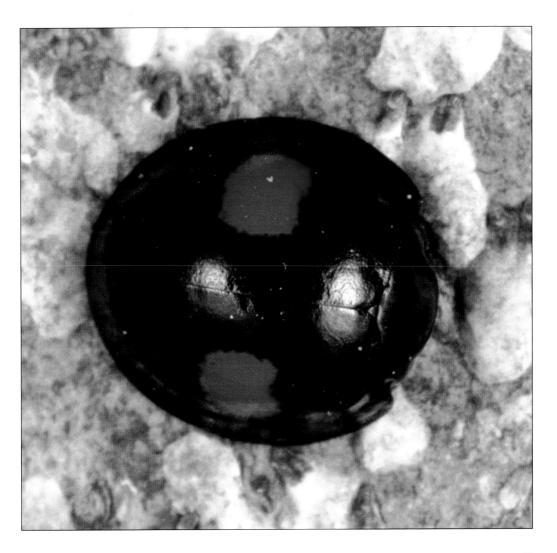

5

Ladybugs have two wings.

---❖---

Las mariquitas tienen dos alas.

Ladybugs have six legs.

❖

Las mariquitas tienen seis patas.

Ladybugs crawl on leaves.

———◆———

Las mariquitas trepan por la hojas.

Ladybugs eat bugs.

❖

Las mariquitas comen insectos.

Ladybugs fly.

❖

Las mariquitas vuelan.

Ladybugs land.

---❖---

Las mariquitas
se posan.

Crawl, ladybug, crawl!

◆

¡Trepa mariquita, trepa!

Words We Know
Palabras conocidas

black spots
manchas negras

bugs
insectos

leaves
hojas

20

legs
patas

red spots
manchas rojas

wings
alas

21

Index

Índice

About the Author

Dana Meachen Rau is an author, editor, and illustrator. A graduate of Trinity College in Hartford, Connecticut, she has written more than one hundred fifty books for children, including nonfiction, biographies, early readers, and historical fiction. She lives with her family in Burlington, Connecticut.

With thanks to the Reading Consultants:

Nanci Vargus, Ed.D., is an Assistant Professor of Elementary Education at the University of Indianapolis.

Beth Walker Gambro received her M.S. Ed. Reading from the University of St. Francis, Joliet, Illinois.

Sobre la autora

Dana Meachen Rau es escritora, editora e ilustradora. Graduada del Trinity College de Hartford, Connecticut, ha escrito más de ciento cincuenta libros para niños, entre ellos libros de ficción histórica y de no ficción, biografías y libros de lectura para principiantes. Vive con su familia en Burlington, Connecticut.

Con agradecimiento a las asesoras de lectura:

Nanci R. Vargus, Dra. en Ed., es profesora ayudante de educación primaria en la Universidad de Indianápolis.

Beth Walker Gambro recibió su Maestría en Ciencias de la Educación, con especialización en Lectura, de la Universidad de St. Francis, en Joliet, Illinois.

Marshall Cavendish Benchmark
99 White Plains Road
Tarrytown, New York 10591-9001
www.marshallcavendish.us

Library of Congress Cataloging-in-Publication Data

Rau, Dana Meachen, 1971–
[Crawl, ladybug, crawl! Spanish & English]
Crawl, ladybug, crawl! = ¡Trepa mariquita, trepa! / by Dana Meachen Rau.
p. cm. – (Go, critter, go! / ¡Vamos criaturita, vamos!)
Includes index.
ISBN-13: 978-0-7614-2817-6 (bilingual edition) – ISBN-13: 978-0-7614-2793-3 (spanish edition)
ISBN-13: 978-0-7614-2652-3 (english edition)
1. Ladybugs–Juvenile literature.
I. Title. II. Title: ¡Trepa mariquita, trepa!
QL596.C65R3818 2007b
595.76'9–dc22
2007013910

Spanish Translation and Text Composition by
Victory Productions, Inc.

Photo Research by Anne Burns Images

Cover Photo by *Peter Arnold Inc.*/PHONE/Jean-Michel Labat

The photographs in this book are used with permission and through the courtesy of:
Peter Arnold Inc.: pp. 1, 19 PHONE/Jean-Michel Labat; pp. 3, 20TL Jean-Jacques Etienne; pp. 7, 21B D. Bringard.
Corbis: pp. 5, 21TR Bob Marsh/Papilio; pp. 9, 21TL Ralph A. Clevenger; pp. 13, 20TR Anthony Bannister/Gallo Images.
Animals Animals: pp. 11, 20B Robert Maier; p. 15 Paulo De Oliveira; p. 17 Stephen Dalton.

Printed in Malaysia
1 3 5 6 4 2